AF382246

MICHELANGELO

An icon of Western art history

Written by Delphine Gervais de Lafond
In collaboration with Angélique Demur
Translated by Rebecca Neal

MICHELANGELO

- **Name:** Michelangelo di Lodovico Buonarroti Simoni, better known as Michelangelo.
- **Born:** 6 March 1475 in Caprese (near Florence).
- **Died:** 18 February 1564 in Rome.
- **Context:** the Italian Renaissance.
- **Notable works:**
  - The *Pietà* in St. Peter's Basilica, Rome (1498-1499), sculpture
  - *David* (1501-1504), sculpture
  - *Doni Tondo* (1506-1508), panel painting
  - The ceiling of the Sistine Chapel (1508-1512), fresco
  - The tomb of Pope Julius II (1504-1545)
  - *The Last Judgment* (1536-1541), fresco

With his mastery of a range of artistic disciplines and insatiable curiosity, the sculptor, architect, painter and poet Michelangelo embodied the ideals of the Renaissance. Unlike his great rival Raphael (Italian painter, 1483-1520), he was a tireless worker and led a solitary, reclusive life, guided by his all-consuming passion for art.

He displayed exceptional artistic talent from a very young age and soon attracted the attention of influential patrons. Throughout his career, he took on a range of prestigious commissions, including the tomb of Pope Julius II and the frescoes adorning the ceiling of the Sistine Chapel in Rome. However, he was frequently dissatisfied with his own work and left a number of his projects unfinished. He produced works across a number of disciplines, gradually shifting his focus from painting and sculpture in the early years of his career to architecture in the later stages of his life.

His monumental works blend traditional and innovative features: to begin with, his work was shaped by his Tuscan heritage, but as time went on he distanced himself from this style to base his architectural and sculptural work on Greco-Roman principles, although he added his own touches to these classical models. He was far ahead of his time and provided an inexhaustible source of inspiration for subsequent generations of artists.

CONTEXT

THE ART OF THE ITALIAN RENAISSANCE

In art history, the Italian Renaissance is traditionally divided into two periods: the Quattrocento (15th century) and the Cinquecento (16th century). The three main artists of the Quattrocento were the architect Filippo Brunelleschi (1377-1446), the sculptor Donatello (c. 1386-1466) and the painter Masaccio (1401-1428); other key figures of this period include Lorenzo Ghiberti (1381-1455), Paolo Uccello (1397-1475), Piero della Francesca (1416-1492) and Andrea Mantegna (1431-1506). The most important figures of the Cinquecento were four artists who each worked across a range of disciplines: Bramante (1444-1514), Leonardo da Vinci (1452-1519), Raphael and Michelangelo. The celebrated painter Sandro Botticelli (1445-1510) was also active during this period. The artistic capital of the Quattrocento was undoubtedly Florence, while Rome was the key hub of the Cinquecento.

The defining characteristic of the Renaissance was the fact that its artists drew thematic and aesthetic inspiration from ancient Greece and Rome, as they read the works of authors from antiquity and took an interest in the archaeological discoveries that uncovered some of the masterpieces of Greek and Roman statuary, including *Laocoön and His Sons* (sculpture, excavated in Rome in 1506) and *Apollo Belvedere* (marble statue, rediscovered in central Italy in the late 15th century). Architects began to apply the theories of Pythagoras (Greek philosopher and mathematician, 6th century BCE) and Vitruvius (Roman architect and engineer, 1st century BCE) to their work, and artists increasingly distanced themselves from the Christian tradition by choosing to depict pagan and secular subjects in their work as well as religious themes, and by taking on commissions from wealthy aristocratic and bourgeois families in addition to those they received from the Church. Scientific and technical advances in fields as diverse as mathematics, astronomy, anatomy and medicine also had a direct impact on the art produced during the Renaissance. Furthermore, the development of mechanical movable type printing by Johannes Gutenberg (1397/1400-1468) in the 1450s facilitated the dissemination of new knowledge throughout Europe.

Finally, doctrines such as humanism and Neoplatonism had a significant influence on architecture, painting and sculpture. According to these schools of thought, humans were created in God's image and were at the centre of the universe, which noticeably affected the arts. For instance, portraits became very fashionable and painters sought to confer greater psychological and anatomical realism on their subjects. They achieved this through the skilful use of light, proportions and perspective, and male nudes were increasingly depicted as representations of divine beauty.

PHILOSOPHY DURING THE RENAISSANCE

Humanism emerged in Italy in the late 14th century, and in its strictest sense, the movement involved studying the original versions of ancient Greek and Roman texts. More broadly, humanism stressed the potential of humankind and its capacity for progress, and promoted education as a source of individual fulfilment.

Neoplatonism was inspired by Plato's (Greek philosopher, c. 427-347 BCE) philosophical doctrines, and emerged in Rome in the 3rd century CE. Its most prominent adherent was Plotinus (c. 205-270), and the movement emphasised the importance of ideas over a sense-based perception of reality. In the 15th century, translations of the writings of Plato and Plotinus reawakened widespread interest in this doctrine, and a Platonic Academy was founded in Florence by Cosimo de' Medici (1389-1464) in 1459. This group was led by the Italian humanist Marsilio Ficino (1433-1499) and counted some of the most illustrious humanist thinkers of the era, including Angelo Poliziano (1454-1494) and Giovanni Pico della Mirandola (1463-1494), among its members.

THE CHANGING STATUS OF THE ARTIST

The concept of the artist as we understand it today emerged during the Renaissance. In the Middle Ages, sculpture and painting were classed among the mechanical arts, alongside manual activities such as goldsmithery, haberdashery, drapery and medicine. It was not until the 15th and 16th centuries that artists began to step out of the shadows, but they needed to attain the title of "master" to have any hope of recognition. To do this, young apprentices joined the workshop of a master from the age of 12 or 13. There, they began by carrying out domestic work (cleaning the workshop, grinding pigments, etc.), before moving on to more technical tasks (preparing the material, painting motifs, etc.) and contributing to the master's work (although they did not work on the more delicate parts, such as hands and faces). It was only after completing this lengthy apprenticeship that they could become masters in their own right.

Art had already attracted the patronage of the upper classes in the Middle Ages, but during the Quattrocento a new generation of patrons emerged and played a major role in the development and spread of Italian culture. Artists in Florence enjoyed the patronage of the Medici family, those in Rome benefitted from the patronage of the popes, and the Montefeltro, Sforza,

Este and Gonzaga families contributed to artistic development in Urbino, Milan, Ferrara and Mantua respectively. All these influential people supported the work of the most celebrated artists of the Renaissance.

The Medicis were a wealthy Florentine banking family who played a crucial role in Michelangelo's development and success as an artist. Lorenzo de' Medici (1449-1492), also known as Lorenzo the Magnificent, followed in the footsteps of his grandfather Cosimo de' Medici and his father Piero di Cosimo de' Medici (c. 1416-1469) by promoting the arts, which greatly contributed to the city's prestige. Under his leadership, Florence enjoyed a golden age and became the cultural centre of the entire Italian peninsula. His palace was an essential meeting point for the city's intelligentsia, as philosophers, poets and artists flocked there to discuss humanism.

THE LIVES OF THE MOST EXCELLENT PAINTERS, SCULPTORS, AND ARCHITECTS

Giorgio Vasari (1511-1574) is widely recognised as the first art historian and theorist of art. In 1550, he published a collection of biographies of the leading artists of the Renaissance titled *The Lives of the Most Excellent Painters, Sculptors, and Architects*, which played a major role in the development of the genre. This book was the first to use the term "Renaissance" to refer to the artistic revolution that was taking place at this time. Vasari was particularly enthusiastic about Michelangelo's work, describing him as the greatest artist, living or dead, and effusively praising his mastery of not one but three artistic disciplines.

BIOGRAPHY

MICHELANGELO AND THE *SCARPELLINI*

Michelangelo di Lodovico Buonarroti Simoni was born in Tuscany on 6 March 1475 to a Florentine family. His father was an administrator of the towns of Chiusi and Caprese. After his mother died when he was six years old, Michelangelo was sent to live with a nurse and her husband, who was a stonemason. According to Vasari, Michelangelo's early love of sculpture came from watching the *scarpellini* (a word derived from the Italian *scalpello* or *scarpello*, meaning chisel; at this time *scarpellare* referred to carving marble) at work.

In 1488, Michelangelo joined the workshop of Domenico Ghirlandaio (1449-1494) for a three-year apprenticeship. During his time there, he studied painting and copied the frescoes of Giotto (c. 1266-1337) and Masaccio, but he left the workshop before the end of his apprenticeship to study sculpture under Bertoldo di Giovanni (c. 1440-1491), who was at the head of a school of young sculptors under the patronage of Lorenzo de' Medici. Medici soon noticed Michelangelo's exceptional talent and invited him to copy the ancient statues in his sculpture garden at San Marco. The young artist was received at the family's palace, where he mingled with some of the most influential men of the time. He also learnt about the principles of Neoplatonism from the humanist philosophers Ficino, Poliziano and Pico della Mirandola.

Between the ages of 15 and 17, Michelangelo sculpted his first reliefs, *Madonna of the Steps* and *Battle of the Centaurs* (1490-1492). In 1494, the death of Lorenzo de' Medici and the arrival of the French army under Charles VIII (1470-1498) forced him to leave the city. After a brief stop in Venice, he spent a year living in Bologna, where he produced statues for the tomb of Saint Dominic.

GREAT PROJECTS

In spite of his youth, by the time he arrived in Rome in June 1496, Michelangelo was already considered to be one of the greatest sculptors of his time thanks to his technical skill and mastery of proportions and anatomy. It was at this time that he completed his famous *Pietà* at St. Peter's Basilica in Rome (1498-1499).

In 1501, after spending five years in Rome, Michelangelo returned to Florence, where he had been commissioned for a number of sculptures, including two bas-reliefs for private clients: the *Taddei Tondo* (1504-1505) and the *Pitti Tondo* (1504-1508). He also produced the *Doni Tondo* (1506-1508), a painting depicting Mary and Jesus, for the Doni family, and was commissioned to paint a fresco of the Battle of Cascina for the Salone dei Cinquecento of the Palazzo Vecchio, although he soon abandoned the project. However, undoubtedly the best-known work from this period in Florence was *David* (1501-1504), which remains his most celebrated sculpture to this day.

In 1505, Michelangelo returned to Rome and was commissioned by Pope Julius II (1443-1513) to work on his tomb. This was a colossal project, as the Pope intended his tomb to be a majestic monument at the centre of St. Peter's Basilica, on the scale of ancient mausoleums. Michelangelo spent eight months in the quarries of Carrara choosing the finest marble, but by the time he returned, the Pope had turned his attentions to another project, namely the construction of St. Peter's Basilica, which had been entrusted to the architect Bramante. Michelangelo was frustrated by the Pope's apparent loss of interest in the previous project and put it on hold while he returned to Florence. He worked on the tomb on and off throughout his career, but it was left unfinished at his death and was such a source of heartache for him that his biographer Ascanio Condivi referred to it as a "tragedy".

In 1508, Julius II summoned Michelangelo back to Rome to paint the frescoes on the ceiling of the Sistine Chapel. This was a monumental project, and the artist spent four years working tirelessly on it, painting suspended from a scaffold several metres above the ground. This uncomfortable position and the speed at which he needed to work exhausted him. He even poked fun at himself in a drawing of himself craning his body upwards with paint dripping down onto him.

In 1520, Pope Julius II's successor, Pope Leo X (1475-1521), who was also the son of Lorenzo de' Medici, sent Michelangelo to Florence to carry out work on the Basilica de San Lorenzo. Specifically, he was to work on the façade (this was never carried out), the tombs in the new sacristy and the library adjoining the building (these two elements were both left unfinished). Michelangelo worked on the basilica on and off until 1534.

When Leo X died in 1521, the new pope, Clement VII (1478-1534), commissioned Michelangelo to work on a library which would features books from Lorenzo de' Medici's collection. The artist quickly completed the vestibule and the imposing three-part staircase before abandoning the project. It was completed by Bartolomeo Ammannati (1511-1592) a few years later. Subsequently, Michelangelo split his time between Florence and Rome and continued working on projects that he had already started. During the 1530s, he became close friends with the artist Tommaso Cavalieri (1509-1587) and the writer Vittoria Colonna (1490-1547).

FINAL YEARS

Michelangelo worked on the last great projects of his life in Rome. In 1532, Clement VII commissioned him to replace the frescoes at the ends of the Sistine Chapel, which had been painted by Pietro Perugino (c. 1448-1523), with two vast scenes: *The Last Judgment* and *The Fall of the Rebel Angels*. After Clement VII died in 1534, his successor, Paul III (1468-1549), wanted to continue with the project, but only *The Last Judgment* (1536-1541) was completed.

The last 20 years of Michelangelo's life were primarily devoted to architecture: he worked on the Piazza del Campidoglio, the Palazzo Farnese, the reconstruction of St. Peter's Basilica based on Bramante's plans, the Basilica of St. Mary of the Angels and the Martyrs, and the Sforza Chapel in the Basilica of Santa Maria Maggiore. However, he continued to sculpt some *Pietà* and painted the frescoes in the Pauline Chapel in the Apostolic Palace in Vatican City (1542-1550). He was greatly weakened by his work, which afforded him very little time to rest, and he died of exhaustion on 18 February 1564. Although Pope Pius IV (1499-1565) wanted him to be buried in St. Peter's Basilica in Rome, his body was transported back to Florence and interred in the Basilica of Santa Croce.

Given Michelangelo's towering reputation as a painter, sculptor and architect, it is often forgotten that he also wrote poetry. In fact, he was the author of over 300 poems, which were published by his great-nephew Michelangelo Buonarroti the Younger (1568-1646) in 1623. Buonarroti allegedly modified some of the pronouns in the poems to conceal the fact that they were written about the artist Tommaso Cavaliere, who was more than 30 years younger than Michelangelo. Consequently, for a long time it was believed that all of his love poems were dedicated to Vittoria Colonna.

CHARACTERISTICS OF MICHELANGELO'S WORK

A MONUMENTAL STYLE

Michelangelo is primarily known for the vast scale of his works. Although he drew inspiration from classical Greco-Roman art, he rejected certain conventions associated with it, such as the prioritisation of balance and symmetry in representations of the human body.

The vast scale of Michelangelo's paintings, sculptures and architectural work gives his buildings and figures a real sense of majesty, although his creations were sometimes criticised for being disproportionate and unnatural, in contrast to the elegance of Raphael's work.

Specifically, in his architectural works he often used the giant order, meaning an architectural order featuring columns that span multiple storeys of a building. In spite of his statues' larger-than-life size, his skilful use of anatomy confers greater life on them and gives them a sense of emotion that is absent in their ancient models. Similarly, the people in his paintings are usually huge in scale and relatively androgynous, with overdeveloped muscles, and his use of contrasting colours makes the scenes he painted seem extraordinarily lifelike and dynamic. Although his paintings were mainly religious in nature, he subtly incorporated secular elements, depicting pagan sibyls alongside Christian prophets.

THE *PIETÀ*

One of Michelangelo's preferred subjects was the *Pietà*. He produced three in total: the *Pietà* of St. Peter's Basilica in Rome (1498-1499), the *Pietà Bandini* (c. 1550) and the *Pietà Rondanini* (c. 1564)

The word *Pietà* is derived from the Latin *pietas*, meaning "piety", and is generally used to refer to depictions of the Virgin Mary cradling Jesus in her arms after his crucifixion. It is a traditional subject in Christian iconography, and is closely linked to the theme of the *Mater Dolorosa* ("Our Lady of Sorrows"), which was widespread in the Middle Ages, particularly in French and Byzantine art.

Of Michelangelo's three *Pietàs*, the one in St. Peter's Basilica in Rome is the most accomplished, although the *Pietà Bandini* is the most original, in both aesthetic and symbolic terms. As well as the traditional Mary and Jesus, it depicts two other figures: Nicodemus supporting Jesus's body and Mary Magdalene crouching on his left. This later work was not a commission, but a sculpture produced for the artist's own tomb, and the figure of Nicodemus is believed to be a self-portrait. The *Pietà Rondanini* was Michelangelo's final sculpture, and he died before he had time to complete it.

THE *TONDI*

A *tondo* (an abbreviation of the Italian word *rotondo*, meaning "round") is a circular painting or bas-relief. A painted *tondo* is generally displayed in a large carved wooden frame.

This circular form first emerged during the Middle Ages and came back into fashion in Italy during the Renaissance, largely due to a resurgence in the popularity of the *desco da parto* ("birth tray"), which was given as a symbolic gift following a successful birth and was often commissioned by wealthy families to mark the birth of their first child. The scenes depicted in these paintings are generally mythological, religious or allegorical in nature and are typically highly symbolic.

Michelangelo produced three famous *tondi*: the bas-reliefs *Taddei Tondo* (1504-1505) and *Pitti Tondo* (1504) and the panel painting *Doni Tondo* (1506-1508). The three works all share the same theme, namely the Virgin and Child.

FRESCOES

Michelangelo's best-known paintings are his frescoes, and the frescoes adorning the ceiling of the Sistine Chapel are among the finest examples of pictorial art from the Italian Renaissance.

The word *fresco* is Italian for "fresh". The technique comprises several steps. After preparing the surface to be painted, the artist draws the outline of their composition on a rough underlayer called the *arriccio*. They then go over the lines of their drawing in a red pigment called sinopia. The next stage is to apply a second layer (made of fine sand or powdered marble mixed with chalk and water) called intonaco, onto which the fresco that will be visible to observers will be painted. The artist must apply the paint when the intonaco is still wet so that the colours will adhere to its surface. This technique is delicate and time-consuming, and leaves no room for hesitation or mistakes.

NOTABLE WORKS

THE *PIETÀ* IN ST. PETER'S BASILICA, ROME

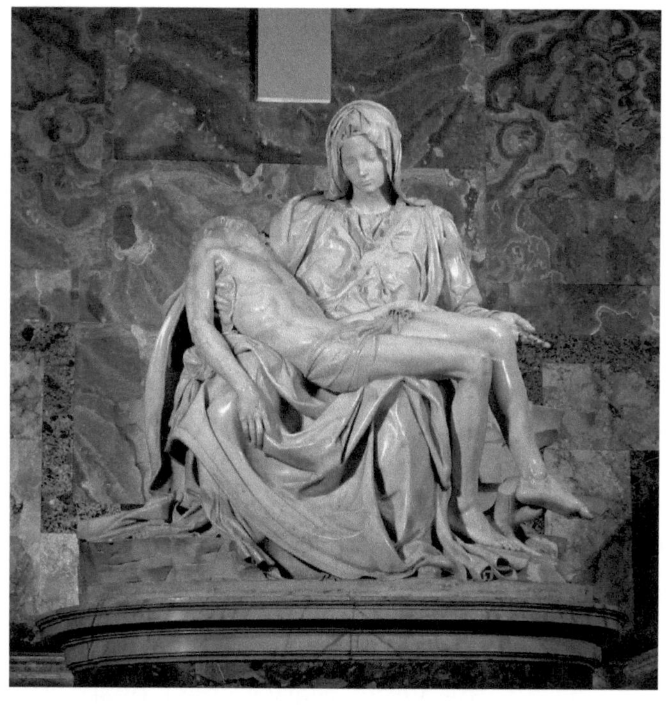

| *Pietà*, 1498-1499, marble statue, 174 x 195 x 69 cm, Rome, St. Peter's Basilica.

In 1497, the French ambassador to Rome, Cardinal Jean Bilhères de Lagraulas (c. 1439-1499), commissioned the 22-year-old Michelangelo to produce a *Pietà*. The sculpture was financed by the banker Jacopo Galli and was intended to feature on the cardinal's funerary monument in the Chapel of the French Kings in the Old St. Peter's Basilica in Rome. Bilhères died shortly after the sculpture was completed.

The finished work is a remarkable achievement, as the life-sized sculpture was carved from a single block of marble from Carrara. The slight tilt of the Virgin Mary's head towards her son's lifeless body conveys her grief, and her face is strikingly beautiful and innocent. The pyramidal composition of the group symbolises the Trinity (the Father, the Son and the Holy Spirit). The sculpture as a whole gives an impression of calm and serenity which is perfectly suited to its religious subject matter.

The piece is also significant because it is the only one of Michelangelo's works that he signed: a sash across the Virgin Mary's chest bears the inscription "MICHAEL.ANGELUS.BONAROTUS. FLORENT.FACIEBAT" ("Michelangelo Buonarroti of Florence Created This"). It is currently displayed in the Chapel of the Pietà in St. Peter's Basilica in Rome.

DAVID

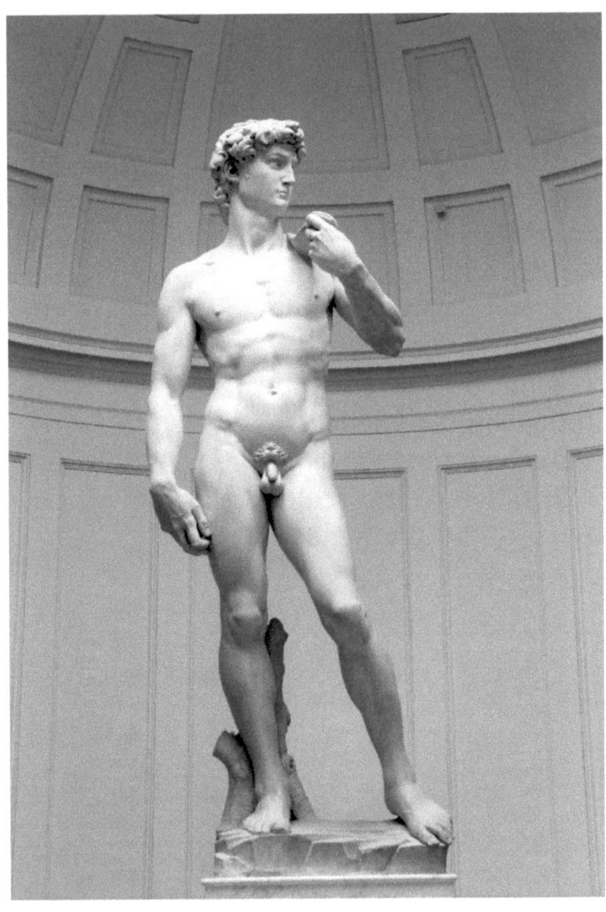

| *David*, 1501-1504, marble statue, 434 cm tall, Florence, Galleria dell'Accademia.

David is undoubtedly Michelangelo's most famous sculpture. Its reputation rests on its exceptional beauty, its size (it is very large for the time it was produced) and Vasari's effusive praise of it. The inspiration for the sculpture is a Biblical episode from the first book of Samuel in which the young shepherd David from the tribe of Judah defeats the Philistine Goliath. David is depicted using *contrapposto* (counterpoise), a posture that was often used in Greek statues in which most of the statue's weight is resting on one leg, before his famous combat. The only element indicating the statue's link to this celebrated episode is the catapult he is holding nonchalantly against his shoulder.

In 1501, the Overseers of the Office of Works of Florence Cathedral were debating what to do with a large rough-hewn block of marble that had been abandoned by previous sculptors. The delicate task of sculpting it was entrusted to the young Michelangelo.

After three years of work, during which the artist hid his work in progress behind a wooden panel, the statue was unveiled and a committee of celebrated artists, including Leonardo da

Vinci and Sandro Botticelli, was tasked with deciding where to place it. The statue's size (over four metres tall) and the fact that it depicts a naked man meant that it could not be placed in the cathedral, so it was decided that it would be displayed in front of the Palazzo Vecchio. It remained there until 1873, when it was transferred to the Galleria dell'Accademia. A copy of the statue now stands in its original location, and there is a second replica in bronze in the Piazzale Michelangelo to the south of the River Arno in Florence.

DONI TONDO

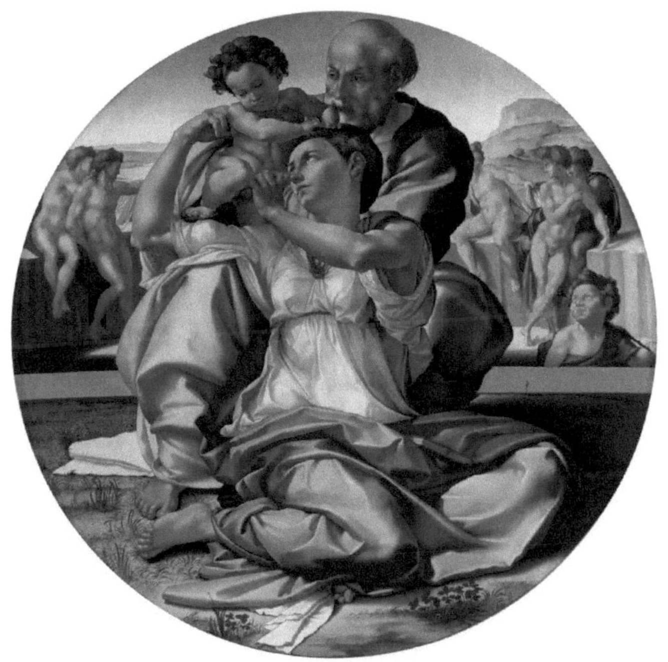

| *Doni Tondo*, 1506-1508, panel painting, 120 cm diameter, Florence, Uffizi Gallery.

The *Doni Tondo* is both the only known example of a painting by Michelangelo on a mobile base and the only of the artist's paintings currently in Florence. It depicts an intimate scene featuring Jesus, Mary and Joseph, with Saint John the

Baptist as a child in the right-hand corner behind the balustrade. However, this seemingly traditional Christian work is in fact highly original, in both stylistic and iconographic terms.

The painting's composition incorporates a spiral effect which draws the viewer's eye towards Jesus, and rather than a traditional triangular composition, it can be described as pyramidal, as the work has a depth which makes the figures depicted exceptionally lifelike and captivating. The chiaroscuro technique used to depict the robes draped over them is a striking testament to Michelangelo's technical skill. The nudes in the background attest to the influence of classical art on Michelangelo's work, while the figure behind Joseph is reminiscent of the famous Greek sculpture *Laocoön and His Sons* (1st century BCE). The coexistence of ancient and Christian figures makes this painting both extremely enigmatic and entirely emblematic of the Renaissance.

The *Doni Tondo* was commissioned by the Florentine merchant Agnolo Doni and his wife Maddalena Strozzi, probably to commemorate the birth of their daughter Maria in 1507. The wooden frame features ornate curves and carved busts, as well as the coat of arms of the Doni family: three half-moons linked by ribbons and surrounded by four lion's heads.

THE CREATION OF ADAM

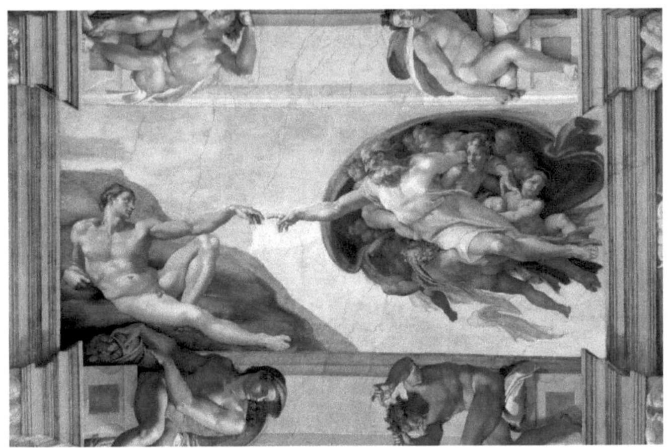

| *The Creation of Adam*, c. 1510-1511, fresco, 270 x 570 cm, Rome, the Sistine Chapel.

The Creation of Adam is one of the nine episodes from Genesis depicted on the ceiling of the Sistine Chapel. Although Michelangelo was initially commissioned to paint the 12 apostles in the pendentives, the finished ceiling instead features numerous key episodes from the Bible, including the Creation, the Great Flood, the story of Noah's Ark and the Fall of Man. There are also *ignudi* (nudes) placed between the central scenes, which shocked viewers at the time.

Between the vaults, there are colossal figures of sibyls and prophets on marble ridges. Four angled pendentives depict scenes related to the salvation of Israel, namely the Nehushtan, the punishment of Haman, the story of David and Goliath and the story of Judith and Holofernes, while the lunettes (situated above the windows) depict the ancestors of Jesus, including Salmon, Josiah, Amos and Hezekiah.

The Creation of Adam is a symbolic interpretation of the passage of the Old Testament "So God created man in his own image" (Genesis 1:27). According to the Bible, God created Adam from the dust of the earth on the sixth day of Creation; however, Michelangelo depicts God breathing life into Adam as though he were turning a marble statue into a flesh and blood being.

The composition features two distinct groups, representing the terrestrial and celestial worlds on the left and right respectively. God is surrounded by angels and wrapped in an extravagant purple cloak, which symbolises his sovereignty, while Adam is alone on the left. He has an athletic physique and his posture is reminiscent of the nudes of antiquity. The composition as a whole converges towards the focal point of the fresco, where God and Adam touch index fingers, thanks to Michelangelo's skilful use of proportions.

MOSES

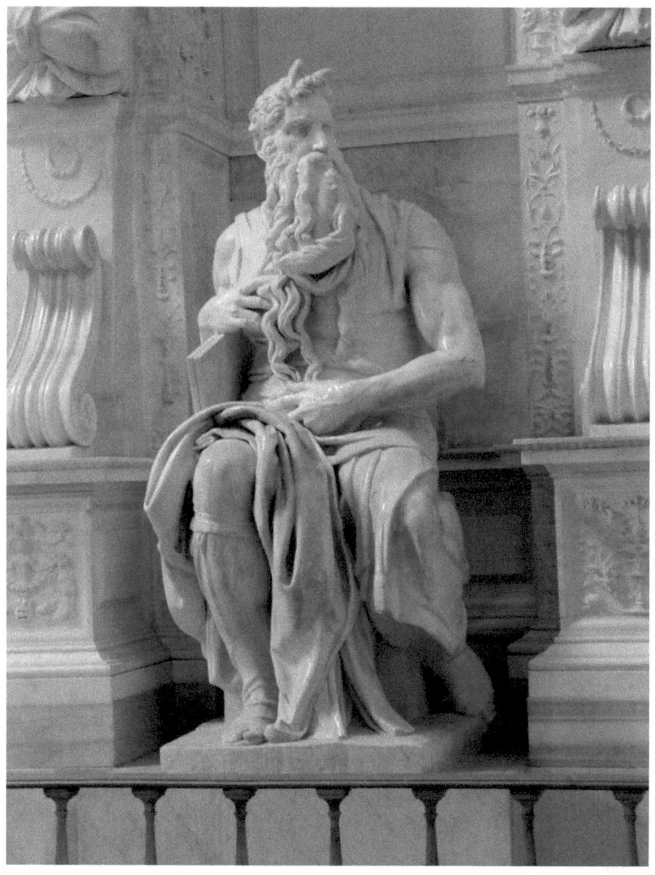

| *Moses*, 1515, marble statue, 235 cm tall, tomb of Pope Julius II, Rome, San Pietro in Vincoli.

The statue of Moses is one of the rare finished elements of Julius II's tomb, which is actually empty, as the pope is buried in St. Peter's Basilica with a simple tombstone. The imposing sculpture, which stands at over two metres tall, is situated in the lower central part of the tomb. Work on the tomb began in 1545, and its two floors also feature sculptures of Rachel, Leah and the Madonna and Child. Michelangelo had initially planned for the tomb to span three floors and house some 40 sculptures. *Moses* was supposed to be placed on the upper level, which was to represent the celestial sphere.

Moses is depicted resting one hand on his stomach, with the other supporting the tablets he received from God and holding back his long, curly beard, and gazing to the left with a preoccupied expression. There was a resurgence of interest in the statue in 1914, when the Austrian psychoanalyst Sigmund Freud (1856-1939) published his essay *The Moses of Michelangelo*, which analyses the depiction of anger in the work.

MOSES WITH HORNS

Moses is depicted with horns due to a mistranslation of Exodus 34: 29-30: "When Moses came down from Mount Sinai with the two tablets of the covenant law in his hands, he was not aware that his face was radiant because he had spoken with the Lord. When Aaron and all the Israelites saw Moses, his face was radiant, and they were afraid to come near him". In the Latin Vulgate translation of this passage, "radiant" is incorrectly rendered as "horns", and as a result many artists in this period depicted Moses with horns.

THE LAST JUDGMENT

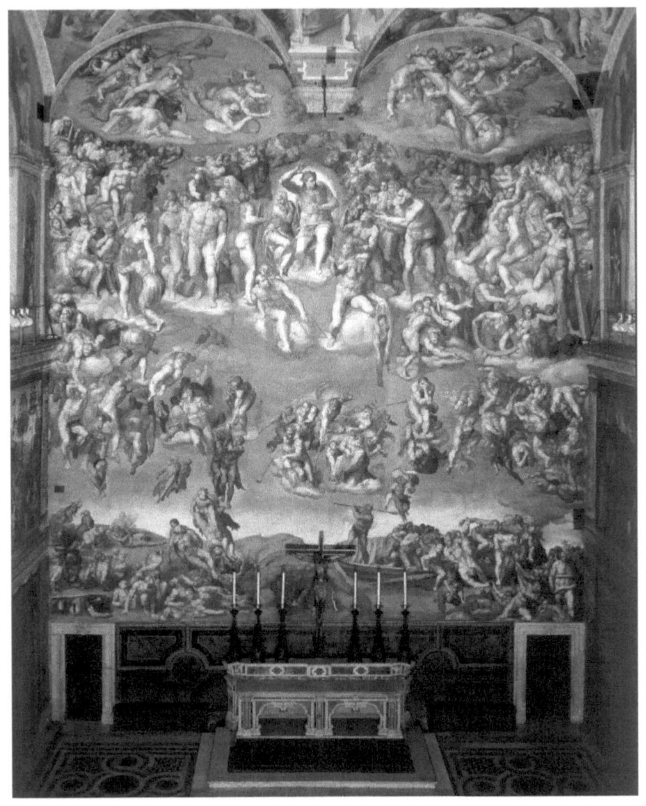

| *The Last Judgment*, 1536-1541, fresco, 1370 x 1220 cm, Rome, the Sistine Chapel.

This vast fresco was commissioned by Pope Clement VII in 1533, shortly before his death. Work on it began three years later, after Paul III was made pope. It was Michelangelo's last contribution to the Sistine Chapel and his final painting.

The painting was inspired by numerous texts from the Old Testament, namely the Gospel of Matthew and the First Epistle to the Corinthians. Many of the figures in the fresco are gazing at Jesus, who is surrounded by a halo of light at the centre of the composition. Mary, to his left (from the observer's point of view), appears resigned, while the saints and the chosen people wait for divine judgment to be proclaimed. Some of them are depicted with their traditional accoutrements (Saint Peter is holding the keys to Paradise, Saint Catherine is carrying the wheel she was sentenced to be broken on, Saint Sebastian's body is pierced with arrows, etc.). It is generally agreed that Michelangelo incorporated a self-portrait into the fresco, depicting his own face on the flayed skin held by Saint Bartholomew. In the lunettes at the top, angels carry symbols of the Passion of Christ: the Cross, the nails used for the crucifixion and the crown of thorns on the left, and the pillar from the Flagellation of Christ, the ladder and the Holy Sponge on the right.

MICHELANGELO'S LEGACY

Two biographies of Michelangelo were published during his lifetime (that of Giorgio Vasari in 1550 and that of his pupil Ascanio Condivi in 1553), which was virtually unheard of at the time and attests to his extraordinary reputation. Both writers contributed to the almost mythical regard in which his talent was held. In the 16th century, numerous Italian admirers sought to emulate his work using exaggerated forms and poses. This movement was known as Mannerism. Michelangelo's influence waned in the 17th and 18th centuries, but there was a major resurgence in interest in his works during the 19th century.

MANNERISM

Mannerism refers to a style of art which flourished between the 1520s and the 1580s, and combines elements of Renaissance and Baroque art. The most important Mannerist painters were Andrea del Sarto (1486-1530) and his pupil Rosso

Fiorentino (1495-1540), Pontormo (1494-1556), Parmigianino (1503-1540), Tintoretto (1518-1594) and El Greco (1541-1614).

Mannerist painters imitated and accentuated the *maniera* ("style") of the great Italian Renaissance artists, namely Michelangelo, Leonardo da Vinci and Raphael. They sought to impart a sense of dynamism to their paintings through exaggerated forms (s-shaped figures), twisted bodies and contrasting colours. Their works were less harmonious than classical models, and they drew a great deal of inspiration from Michelangelo, paying homage to him in a number of extravagant paintings. In the following century, Gian Lorenzo Bernini (1598-1680) and Francesco Borromini (1599-1667) pushed Mannerism even further to create a new style, which became known as Baroque.

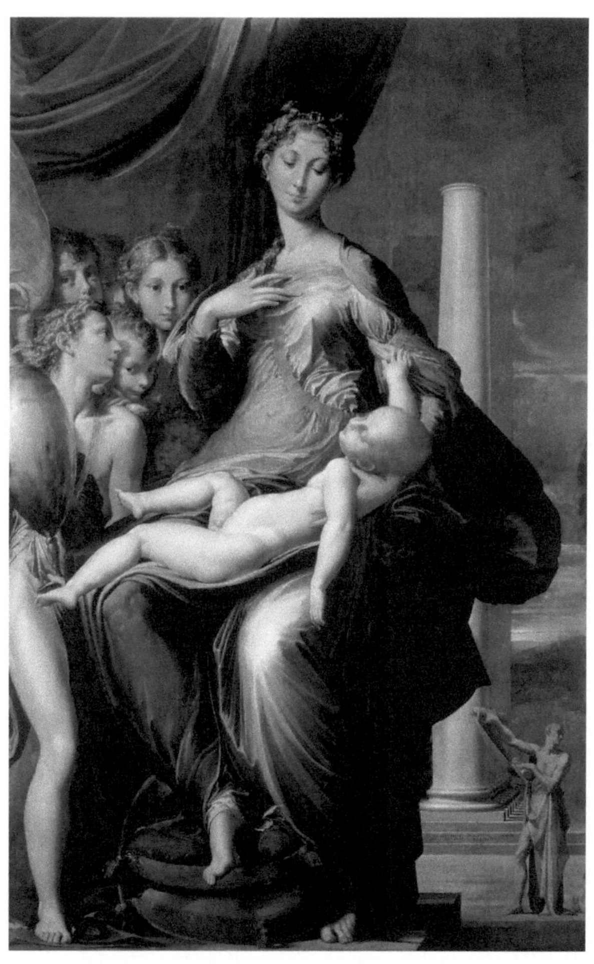

Parmigianino, *Madonna with the Long Neck*, c. 1534-1539, oil painting on wood, 219 x 135 cm, Florence, Uffizi Gallery.

Parmigianino's painting *Madonna with the Long Neck* (c. 1534-1539), which was produced for a church in Parma but left unfinished at his death, clearly demonstrates the extent of Michelangelo's influence in 15th-century Italy. The work can be described as a reinterpretation of the *Pietà* in St. Peter's Basilica, but whereas Michelangelo's structure embodies elegance and piety, the artificiality of Parmigianino's work stands in contrast to the classical ideal.

MICHELANGELO IN THE 19TH CENTURY

Michelangelo's popularity saw a resurgence in the 19th century, and he became a model for a generation of French artists who emphasised modernity in their works, including Jean-Auguste-Dominique Ingres (1780-1867), Théodore Géricault (1791-1824), Eugène Delacroix (1798-1863), August Rodin (1840-1917) and Jean-Baptiste Carpeaux (1827-1875). Romantic artists were inspired by him as they sought greater freedom in their work and broke free of artistic conventions.

The Prix de Rome, which aimed to recognise the best French artist active at that time, also played a role in the rediscovery of Michelangelo's work, as the winner received a bursary allowing them to live in Italy for two to four years so that they could study the great masterpieces of antiquity and the Renaissance. Numerous French painters, architects and sculptors were captivated by Michelangelo's imposing statues and the vast frescoes in the Sistine Chapel, and brought back sketches from their stay in Rome. As an example, the influence of *The Last Judgment* can be clearly seen in Géricault's painting *The Raft of the Medusa* (1818-1819), which was exhibited at the 1819 Paris Salon. The sculptors Carpeaux and Rodin were particularly marked by their stay in Italy, and when they returned to France they produced copies of some of Michelangelo's works and emulated his style in highly personal compositions. Indeed, during his first stay in Italy in 1857, Carpeaux stated that all his works were influenced by Michelangelo.

Rodin first discovered Michelangelo at the Louvre, where the statues of slaves that had been produced for Pope Julius II's tomb were on display. In 1875, he embarked on a kind of pilgrimage to Florence to mark the 400th anniversary of the artist's birth. He was particularly influenced by the emotion and energy of Michelangelo's sculptures, as well as his *non finito* ("unfinished") aesthetic, which he emulated in his own work. Michelangelo's influence can be seen in particular in his depictions of Caryatids, Titans and Atalanta. A number of Rodin's sculptures imitate the poses of Michelangelo's statues, such as *The Age of Bronze* (1877), which is reminiscent of *The Dying Slave* (1513-1516). Also worth mentioning is Rodin's *The Gates of Hell* (1880-1890), which was exhibited at the 1881 Paris Salon and which depicts Adam with a similarly muscular physique and in a similar pose to Michelangelo's Adam in *The Creation of Adam*.

SUMMARY

- Michelangelo was born in 1475 near Florence. He excelled across a number of artistic disciplines, including architecture, sculpture, painting and poetry, but was never satisfied with his own efforts and left a number of works unfinished.
- He had connections to the powerful Medici family and accepted commissions from a wide range of patrons, including several popes. His most important commissions include the tomb of Pope Julius II and the ceilings of the Sistine Chapel in Rome, and the tombs in the new sacristy and the library at the Basilica de San Lorenzo in Florence.
- One of Michelangelo's favourite subjects was the *Pietà*. He produced three of them, the best-known of which is housed in St. Peter's Basilica in Rome (1498-1499) and is the only work he signed. He also produced three *tondi*, including the *Doni Tondo* (1506-1508), all three of which represent the Madonna and Child. However, his reputation as a painter is based largely on his frescoes.

- His style can be described as "monumental", as the scale of his sculptures, paintings and architectural work gives his figures and buildings a sense of majesty. His understanding of anatomy allowed him to give his statues a greater sense of life and emotion, as can be seen in his most famous sculpture *David* (1501-1504). Similarly, in his paintings he used sharply contrasting colours to make the scenes he depicted more vivid and dynamic. In all his works, the figures he created were large and androgynous, with very muscular physiques.
- Michelangelo is considered the father of Mannerism, an artistic movement which emerged in Italy in the 16th century and involved exaggerating the style of the great Italian Renaissance masters. He inspired many subsequent artists, including Auguste Rodin and a number of other 19th-century French sculptors.

We want to hear from you!
Leave a comment on your online library
and share your favourite books on social media!

FURTHER READING

BIBLIOGRAPHY

- Arasse, D. (1981) L'index de Michel-Ange. *Communications*. 34. pp. 6-24.

- Boissière A. (2006) Interprétation et expérience vécue dans *Le Moïse* de Michel-Ange : Freud et Theodor Reik. *Savoirs et Clinique*. 7. pp. 39-50.

- Brion, M. and Whitall, J. (2013) *Michelangelo*. Whitefish: Literary Licensing, LLC.

- Cecchi, A. (1987) Les cadres ronds de la Renaissance florentine. Trans. Blamoutier, N. *Revue de l'art*. 76. pp. 21-24.

- Chaix, G. (2002) *La Renaissance, des années 1470 aux années 1560*. Paris: CNED-SEDES.

- Chastel, A. (1983) *The Sack of Rome, 1527*. Trans. Archer, B. Princeton: Princeton University Press.

- Clark, K. (1976) *The Nude*. London: Penguin.

- Comar, P. ed. (2008) *Figures du corps. Une leçon d'anatomie à l'École des beaux-arts*. Paris: ENSBA.

- Condivi, A. (2006) *The Life of Michelangelo*. Trans. Holroyd, C. London: Pallas Athene.

- Crouzet-Pavan, É. (2007) *Renaissances italiennes (1380-1500).* Paris: Albin Michel.

- De Tolnay, C. (1943-1960) *Michelangelo.* 5 vols. Princeton: Princeton University Press.

- Freud, S. (1955) The *Moses* of Michelangelo. In: *The Standard Edition of the Complete Psychological Works of Sigmund Freud.* Vol. XIII (1913-1914): *Totem and Taboo* and Other Works. Trans. Strachey, J. London: Hogarth Press, pp. 211-238.

- Fromentin, E-D. (1997) Jean-Baptiste Carpeaux, Essai biographique. La vie, l'œuvre du statuaire valenciennois d'après sa correspondance. *Valentiana.* Revue d'histoire des pays du Hainaut français. 19.

- Hall, M. B. (2002) *Michelangelo: The Frescoes of the Sistine Chapel.* New York: Abrams Books.

- Lang, J. and Lemoine, C. (2012) *Michel-Ange.* Paris: Fayard.

- (2012) *Michel-Ange au siècle des Carpeaux.* Valenciennes, Musée des Beaux-Arts, 16 March-1 July 2012. [Exhibition catalogue]. Milan: Silvana Editoriale.

- Michelangelo. (2000) *The Complete Poems of Michelangelo.* Trans. Nims, J. F. Chicago: University of Chicago Press.

- Murray, L. (1984) *Michelangelo: His Life, Work and Times.* London: Thames & Hudson.

- Panofsky, E. (1972) *Renaissance and Renascences in Western Art*. London: HarperCollins.

- (1996) *Rodin e Michelangelo*. Florence, Casa Buonarroti, 11 June-16 September. [Exhibition catalogue]. Milan: Charta.

- Sala, C. (2001) *Michel-Ange. Sculpteur, peintre, architecte*. Paris: Éditions Pierre Terrail.

- Vasari, G. (2008) *The Lives of the Artists*. Trans. Conaway Bondanella, J. and Bondanella, P. Oxford: Oxford University Press.

- Wallace, W. E. (2008) *The Treasures of Michelangelo*. London: André Deutsch.

ICONOGRAPHIC SOURCES

- *Pietà*, 1498-1499, marble statue, 174 x 195 x 69 cm, Rome, St. Peter's Basilica. Royalty-free reproduction picture.

- *David*, 1501-1504, marble statue, 434 cm tall, Florence, Galleria dell'Accademia. Royalty-free reproduction picture.

- *Doni Tondo*, 1506-1508, panel painting, 120 cm diameter, Florence, Uffizi Gallery. Royalty-free reproduction picture.

- *The Creation of Adam*, c. 1510-1511, fresco, 270 x 570 cm, Rome, the Sistine Chapel. Royalty-free reproduction picture.

- *Moses*, 1515, marble statue, 235 cm tall, tomb of Pope Julius II, Rome, San Pietro in Vincoli. Royalty-free reproduction picture.

- *The Last Judgment*, 1536-1541, fresco, 1370 x 1220 cm, Rome, the Sistine Chapel. Royalty-free reproduction picture.

- Parmigianino, *Madonna with the Long Neck*, c. 1534-1539, oil painting on wood, 219 x 135 cm, Florence, Uffizi Gallery. Royalty-free reproduction picture.

www.50minutes.com

Ebook EAN: 9782808011266

Paperback EAN: 9782808011273

Legal Deposit: D/2018/12603/308

Cover: © Detail from *The Creation of Adam* by Michelangelo.

Digital conception by Primento, the digital partner of publishers.